Follow the simple step-by-step guides to create lots of wonderful results! Find out how to make a paper pirate hat, a scary Halloween puppet and much more.

LET'S GET STARTED!

THOMAS the tiger

1 Pencil in two circles for the eyes on the paper bag and use scissors to cut them out.

2 Cut off both handles and cut arches on either side.

3 Use a black marker pen to draw on the nose and mouth.

4 Draw in the tiger's stripes and colour them black.

5 Add a pink tongue, ears and orange colouring.

6

CONTENTS

WHAT YOU NEED

The crafts in this book use materials that you can find in art shops, stationers and around your home. This page shows you the materials you will need to make the ideas in this book.

Glue stick

Pencil

Marker pens

Scissors

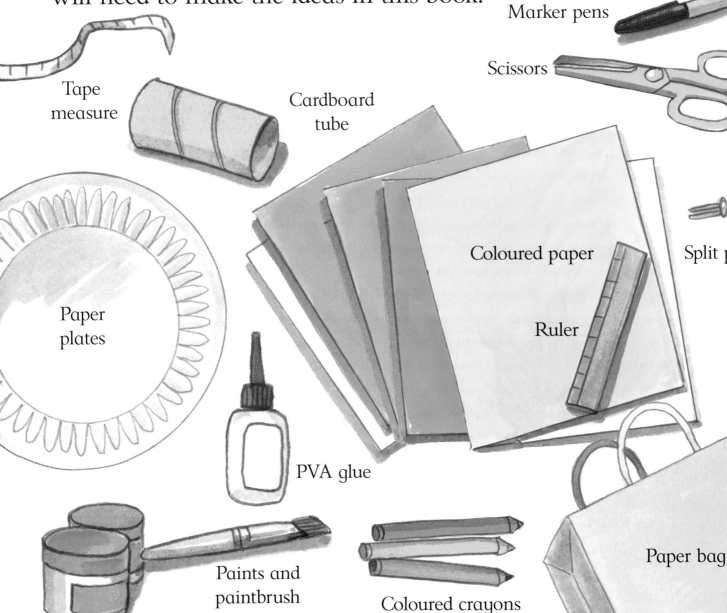

Tape measure

Cardboard tube

Coloured paper

Split pin

Paper plates

Ruler

PVA glue

Paper bag

Paints and paintbrush

Coloured crayons

Snarl!

Snarl!

NOW PUT IT ON YOUR
HEAD AND GROWL
LIKE A TIGER!

7

FELICITY
the fish

1 Fold a sheet of paper (as shown).

2 Cut off the excess to make a folded triangle.

3 Open out flat again. Fold into the centre and crease.

4 Now repeat on the opposite side.

5 Open out flat to show the creases.

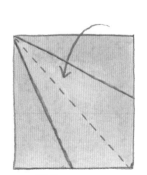

6 Fold at centre to make a triangle shape again.

7 Cut folded edge to the crease (as shown).

8

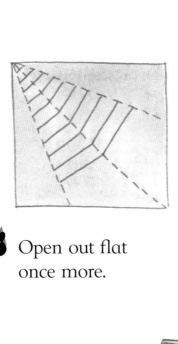

8 Open out flat once more.

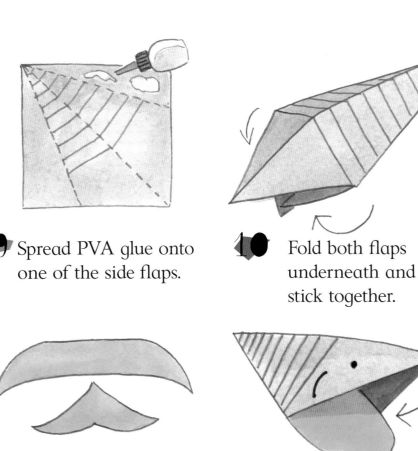

9 Spread PVA glue onto one of the side flaps.

10 Fold both flaps underneath and stick together.

11 Cut shapes from thin coloured card for the tongue, fin and tail.

12 Glue the tongue inside the 3D fish.

13 Now glue on the fins. Use a marker pen to add details.

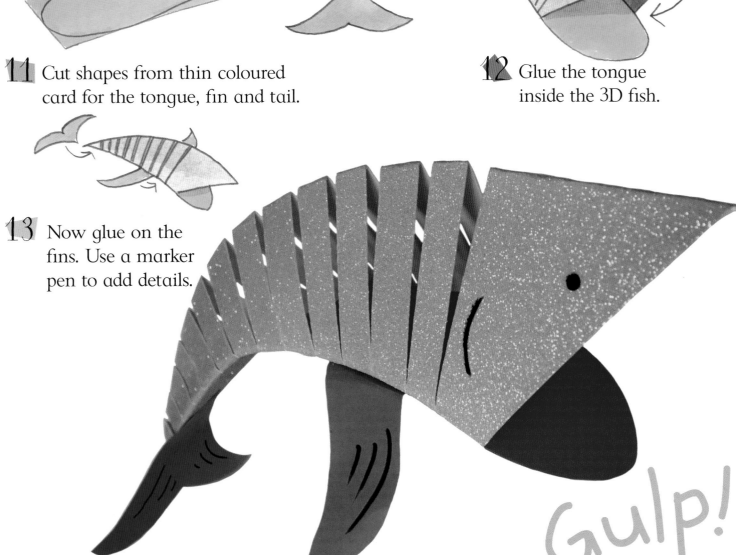

Gulp!

9

TICK-TOCK clock

1 Draw a small arrow and a big arrow on thick red paper. Cut out.

2 Use a pencil to mark the centre of a paper plate.

3 Cut twelve small circles of coloured paper. Number them 1-12.

4 Glue on numbers 12, 3, 6 and 9 (as shown).

5 Now glue on the rest of the numbers in order.

6 Push a split pin through both arrows and fix to the centre of your clock.

Tick tock

DAPHNE the dragon

1 Use a pencil to copy this dragon shape (above).

2 Carefully cut out your dragon.

3 Concertina-fold the centre section.

Swoop!

4 Cut out and glue on a row of sharp teeth and one eye. Using a red marker pen, draw on spots (as shown).

5 Glue a thick cardboard stick behind each leg to make your dragon into a puppet!

Roar!

13

GUSTAV
the whale

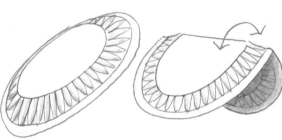

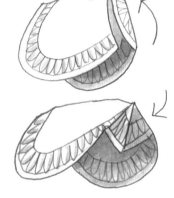

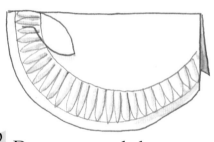

1 Turn a paper plate over and fold in half.

2 Fold one corner over. Reverse the fold to turn it inwards.

3 Draw an oval shape for the tail fins.

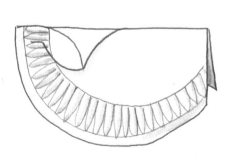

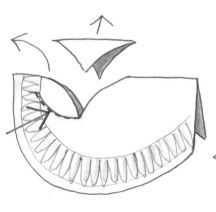

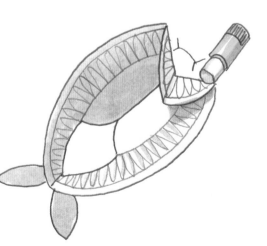

4 Draw another curved line (as shown).

5 Cut off the top section. Cut through the pencil line. Fold both fins out.

6 Glue the folded inset together to make the whale's head.

7 Use a black marker pen to draw in the whale's eye and bill. Cut out the shape of its mouth.

8 Cut out two side fins. Glue on. Cut a small triangle for a blowhole.

9 Fold a piece of paper. Now cut (as shown) towards the folded edge.

Folded edge

10 Roll up this comb-shaped strip and glue it together.

11 Glue the waterspout inside the blowhole.

Splash!

12 Use coloured pencils and paint to colour in your whale.

15

PUMPKIN
hand puppet

1 Fold a piece of A4 paper in half. Now in half again (as shown).

2 Fold (as shown), so sections 1 and 4 meet. Pencil in an oval.

3 Use a black pencil to draw a nose, mouth, eyes and a stalk.

4 Draw in the grooved pumpkin's shape. Now add colour!

5 Open flat. Draw two lines in the folds to make a gaping mouth.

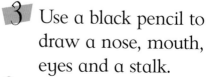

6 Now colour in the folds (as shown). Then use your scissors to cut two strips of paper. Make a folded flap at each end.

7 Turn over your pumpkin puppet. Glue each strip to the back of the folded section (as shown).

Boo!

YOU COULD MAKE LOTS OF OTHER PUPPETS — WHAT ABOUT A SKELETON?

17

FANG
the scary monster

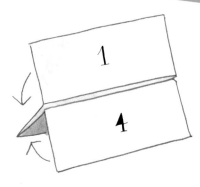

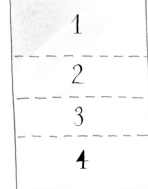

1 Fold a piece of A4 paper in half.

2 Fold it in half again. Lay it out flat.

1
2
3
4

3 Fold so sections 1 and 4 meet.

1
4

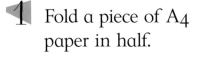

4 Start drawing your monster with its mouth at the centre.

5 Make your monster look harmless so it will only be scary when it opens up!

6 Open out flat. Draw the scary bits in the folded section now.

18

Gurgle!

7 Colour your monster
using coloured pencils.

Rawr!

19

PIRATE HAT

Shiver me timbers!

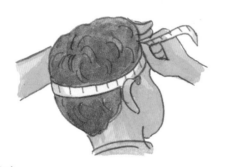

1 First measure the size of your head.

2 Cut and glue a band of black paper to fit your head size.

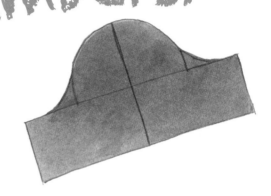

3 Use a pencil to draw a pirate hat shape on thick black paper.

4 Turn the hat over. Glue red tissue paper to the back.

5 Glue the paper band to the back.

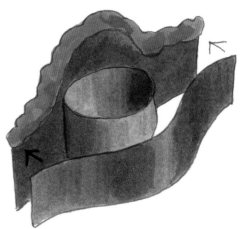

6 Cut another strip of black paper. Glue on to each side of your hat (as shown).

7 Draw an overlapping circle and square on white paper.

8 Draw the eyes and nose (as shown). Use a black marker pen.

9 Now draw in the shape of the skull and cut out.

10 Draw and cut out two bone shapes.

11 Glue the skull and crossbones on to the front.

Walk the plank!

Arrrgh!

DONALD the dinosaur

Dinosaur plates

Pentagons

3 Glue the dinosaur plates to the inside edge of one of the paper plate sides.

2 Draw five pentagons for the dinosaur's plates, and shapes for its head and tail. Cut them out.

1 Fold a paper plate in half and crease.

Roar! Roar!

Thud!

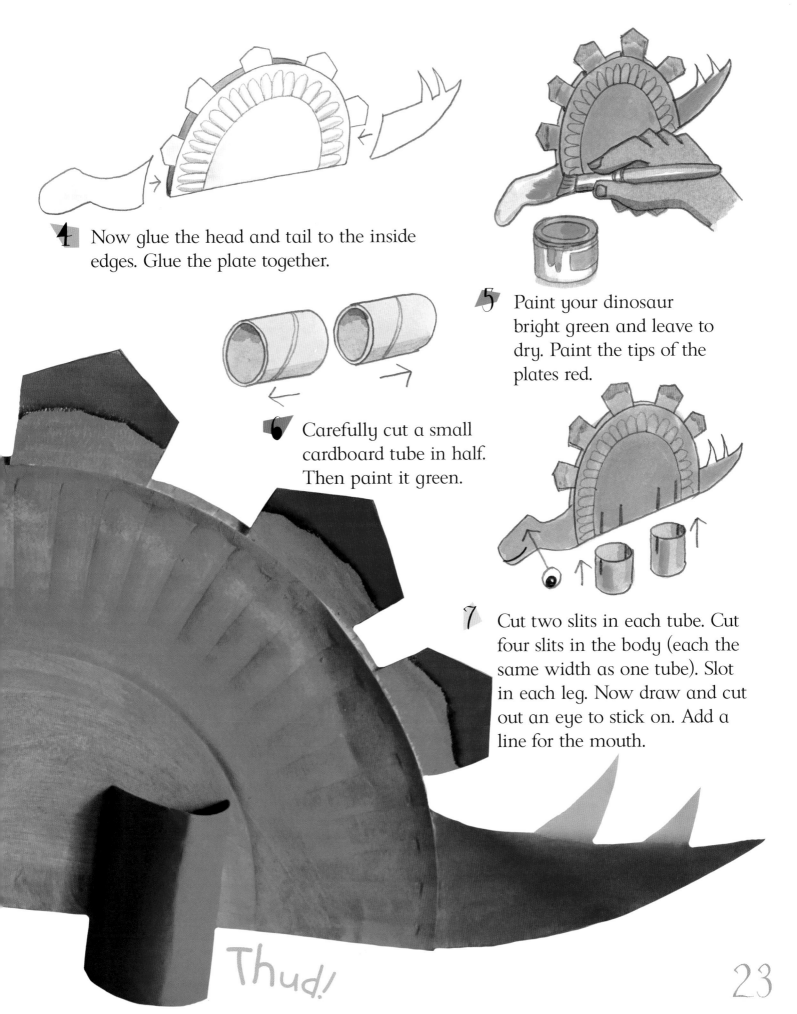

4 Now glue the head and tail to the inside edges. Glue the plate together.

5 Paint your dinosaur bright green and leave to dry. Paint the tips of the plates red.

6 Carefully cut a small cardboard tube in half. Then paint it green.

7 Cut two slits in each tube. Cut four slits in the body (each the same width as one tube). Slot in each leg. Now draw and cut out an eye to stick on. Add a line for the mouth.

Thud!

FRANK
the octopus

1 Using a ruler, pencil in a horizontal line. Now draw nine equally-spaced vertical lines.

2 Use your ruler and pencil to draw long triangles in each vertical strip.

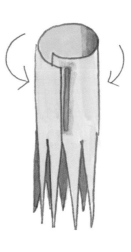

3 Carefully cut out the triangular shapes with scissors (as shown).

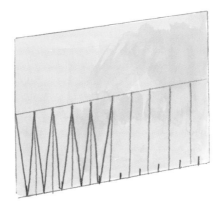

4 Make and stick on two googly eyes.

5 Use a red marker pen to draw suckers onto each octopus arm! Now draw in the mouth.

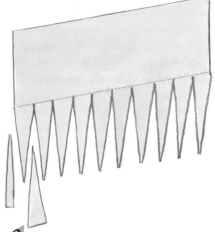

6 Curl your octopus into a cylinder shape and glue the ends together.

24

7 Curl its arms upwards
so it sits up.

GL**OO**P!

BOOKMARKS

Don't lose your place!

1 Cut A4 paper into 20cm strips.

2 Cut one end into a rounded shape.

3 Draw and cut a semi-circle shape about three-quarters of the way up.

4 Draw in your design using a pencil.

5 Colour your bookmarks using crayons or felt tips.

TRY DIFFERENT DESIGNS, PERHAPS INSPIRED BY THE BOOK YOU ARE READING!

Wooooooo!

27

THEO
the lion

Roar!

Growl!

1 Stack together a sheet of yellow, orange and brown paper.

2 Cut the three-coloured stack into narrow strips.

3 Pull the strips over a table edge to make them curly.

4 Glue the strips around an oval shape drawn on coloured board.

5 Pencil in two overlapping circles on orange paper.

6 Use a marker pen to draw in the lion's face, eyes and ears (as shown).

7 Cut out the lion's head with scissors.

8 Glue the lion's face inside the mane using PVA glue.

SANTA tree decoration

Ho Ho Ho!

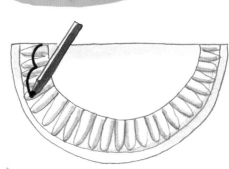

1 Turn a paper plate upside down.

2 Now bend it in half and crease.

3 Draw in the shape of Santa's beard.

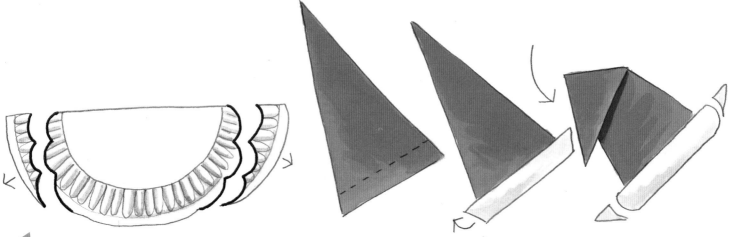

4 Cut off the excess using scissors.

5 Cut a long triangle, out of red paper.

6 Fold the point down. Add a white paper strip to the base (as shown).

7 Cut out Santa's pink face and glue it onto the paper plate.

8 Draw the eyes and mouth. Make and glue on a nose.

9 Glue on his hat.

10 Cut out a white pom-pom shape to glue onto his hat.

ADD STRING TO HANG UP YOUR DECORATION

31

GLOSSARY

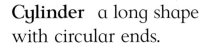

Cylinder a long shape with circular ends.

Base the bottom of something, such as a shape or object.

Blowhole the nostril of a whale or dolphin, located on top of its head, through which it breathes when at the water's surface.

Mane the fur around the face of some animals, such as a lion.

Marker pen a pen containing ink. They come in many different colours.

Pentagon a geometric shape with five sides.

PVA glue a type of glue that is safe for use in arts and crafts activities. It can be used to stick together materials like paper and wood.

Split pin a metal fastener used to join things together.

INDEX